THE GROW JOURNAL

Here You Grow Again

30 DAYS OF SELF AWARENESS

Latonya Denise Atkinson

A Letter from Author **Latonya Denise**

Welcome to the best 30 days of the rest of your life! You should be proud (I know I am) of yourself for taking an initiative to learn, understand and care for yourself. What better place can you imagine than a journey to becoming a better you. What you should appreciate most about this journey is, it is all about YOU! It is YOU learning YOU, while focusing on YOU to better understand YOU. In other words, you can be selfish without any conviction.

This journal was created as a space for YOU to be honest with yourself in hopes to help you grow healthy in your thoughts, behaviors and actions in order to discover the most efficient YOU! The journey will require tons of self-evaluation and accountability. However, it's okay, you won't be graded, not by anyone else at least. Consequently, rewards are plentiful when you are able to look back and observe the GROWTH you've had. You will be willing and excited to share your new and improved self to the people who have tolerated YOU. Don't play, you know you need it.

So, take deep breath in and then exhale. Now let's began traveling to your GROWTH!

Again, welcome and good luck on your journey.

Disclaimer

For those of you who are serious about your new journey to self-awareness please consider this disclaimer.

This journal is not a cure nor has it been tested or proven to serve as a remedy to assist or support any forms mental/emotional health issues. This journal should not be used as a substitute nor intervention for any mental or emotional diagnosis.

Self-awareness in the purest form can cause you to consider and inevitably to conclude hard unknowns about yourself. These conclusions or findings have the potential to manifest and become personal attributes. Personal image can derive from satisfying and dissatisfying discoveries. However, these personal truths, can be techniques used to create change. It is recommended that you practice affirming exercises to support self-worth during this journey. Do not underestimate the possible effects of your truths. And although it should free you from certain bondage, even the truth can come with a price.

Do not be discouraged. Remember you are striving to grow in your personal life and growth pains may be necessary for this process. Self-awareness is just another tool to support your personal advancement.

I recommend you research symptoms of depression, anxiety and other associated mental health and emotional issues.

If you have symptoms that identify with the likes of any mental or emotional issues, I personally recommend you to seek professional counsel.

Self-Awareness Pre-Assessment

Directions: Answer each question to the best of your ability. Be honest with yourself as much as you know how. Remember, no one is grading you but YOU.

I am likely to be angry

when____

I am likely to be sad

when____

I am likely to be happy

when____

I find confidence in my ability to

____

I'm usually at my best

when____________________________

In your own words, define the word, **Faith.**

____

____

____

____

Choose the best answer.

I am a person of

- o Strong Faith
- o Little Faith
- o I am not defined by any faith

Check all that apply.

I am most likely to accept advice from someone who is

- o A keep it real type person
- o A credible, experienced person
- o A "catchy" or able to catch my attention

Insert one word in the blank that best describes you.

I am overly ______________________________.

Explain your answer from the previous response.

How:

____

When:

____

Why:

____

Choose only one answer.

I choose to…

- Get things done on my own.
- Have support or an accountability partner.
- Work with teams of people.

My social of friends …

- Mirror me (we are mostly alike)
- Are primarily different
- Is diverse (includes differences and similarities)

The worst thing that has ever happened to me is…

- my fault
- someone I trusted fault
- just simply the wrong place, wrong time or someone else's fault

I would most likely use my life experiences…

- to avoid making mistakes
- to help others
- I have never taken time to consider

Insert one word in the blank that best describes you.

My biggest fear is

____

Agree or Disagree

- I am aware that I have imperfections. ______
- My imperfections are not designed to teach me. ______
- I have yet to learn everything about me. ______
- I spend less time thinking about my imperfections and more time trying to be productive. ______
- I know that I can accomplish any goal that I choose. ______
- I have more ex-friends than current friends. ______
- I can be cordial with anyone, no matter what has happened between us. ______
- I don't have a circle of friends. ______

You have completed your pre-self-assessment.

In this section, you will find where you will be journaling your GROWTH. This section will be found after each reading. It is provided as a prompt to invoke your writing as you make observations about yourself. Look forward to this section each day as you will have many Growth Moments!

Who Am I: Was there a specific section of the pre-assessment that gave you hesitance? Talk about this area of sensitivity. Why was it so sensitive for you? How do you feel about touching on this subject in the future?

Affirmation: I am on a personal journey to be more self-aware and I will grow into the person I desire to see.

GROWTH MOMENT: Use this section to talk about what your expectations are after completing this journal. What changes would you like to see in yourself?

Let's Get to Growing!

1
CAMOUFLAGE

I am sad with people who always go along, just to get along. I don't mean sad to an extreme, but we all know someone who never has an opinion or input to offer. If you are this person, why do you think you are this way? Have you ever considered it may be because you are way too comfortable with CAMOUFLAGING? Most people who camouflage use the "I don't like conflict" justification. Yes, I believe some people want to avoid conflict, but this reasoning is overly used and unnecessary.

This is a common fear, and it should be addressed within you.

Being a part of a group that has common interests and goals does not mean you necessarily have all things in common. It also does not mean you are without independent opinion or reckoning. Independence does not diminish identity, it establishes it. This is also seen in our families. There are several members of your family, but not all members have the same passions, motivations, or goals. You probably have more differences than similarities, but that doesn't make you any less related. The ability to be different is overlooked and often taken for granted. The fact that every single human does not behave, or respond the same is why sharing the world with others

is tolerable. Can you imagine how boring or dreadful it would be to live in a place where everyone is just like you?

I have met some pretty awesome people. Likewise, I have met some people that were not so awesome. Whether pleasant or not, I remember all individuals especially when they stand out from the crowd. Deciphering whether the individual was seeking my attention at the moment or simply being themselves is not for me to decide. The point is they are remembered for being individualized and different.

How a person wants to be remembered is solely a personal matter. It's not likely an individual will consider how they want to be remembered before every interaction they involve themselves in. Although, if there was a consideration of this sort, we would never make mistakes or wrong impressions. And since no one is perfect, mistakes are needed for growth. You have heard it said that true colors reveal themselves. Maybe you heard it this way, "everything will eventually come to the light." I think you get my point now. I do believe, there are times when some of us decide to just *go along to get along*. Or just simply camouflage.

If you choose to always go along to get along, you may have experienced a time when you were singled out because you didn't agree with the majority. Or maybe you just didn't agree with anyone in the majority. This likely made you perceive this isolated occurrence negatively. It may have caused you to decide to keep your mouth closed and your opinion to yourself onwards. Well, let me inform you of something. The majority may need you to say something. Your silence was once respected, but now your voice is requested. Speak UP! There are times to shut up, but how will you learn if you never say anything. Besides, it's getting pretty annoying to those who value your opinion. I understand the repercussions of saying the wrong thing at the wrong time, but there are also times when something can be resolved if you just open your mouth.

Now that you have a better understanding of speaking up, let's discuss the company you keep. More than likely, you choose to associate with those you have the most in common with. Yes, it is important we surround ourselves with positive, ambitious people who have goals and aspirations as we do, but this doesn't mean you will always agree. And disagreements aren't always deal-breakers. Not with real friends, anyhow. Friends do have a lot in common. They support each other's differences and find reasons to celebrate one another. They are supporters, but not always role models. They should complement your life. Our friends are like crayons. They are so similar to each other, but as they are the same, they should be just as different. They have their special purpose with none needing to be the same color. But when all are on one accord, they can make a bright and colorful portrait. Each standing out where it should.

Your differences are appreciated by the right people. I was advised some time ago that you can please some people at certain times, but

it is rare to please every person at all times. (I know you read that again because I had to say it a few times myself). With this in mind, remember liberty has its limits. But when you are with the right group of people, your opinion will be as respected as you are. If you are a part of any group that does not respect you, your opinion will never matter. Your opinion is not always warranted, and it doesn't always have to be expressed. Only when the subject compromises your dignity and character is when your opinion is the best and correct answer.

You now know you are made to stand out and should never go along just to get along. You can stop with the camouflaging. It wasn't attractive anyhow.

Day Journaling

Who am I?

Do I fear being singled out?

Affirmations: I dare to become the ME that I want to become.

Grow Moment

Reflect on a time when you should have spoken up, but you didn't.

Journal the changes you would like to see.

____

____

____

____

____

Wow, Look at you GROW!

2
Your Message

If you were asked to talk about yourself, you would respond by stating your accomplishments, goals, and probably every kind of service you have ever done for someone. It's highly unlikely you would mention anything you aren't proud of. The reason you were most likely to answer with all of the positive things about yourself is that, as humans, that is what we like others to believe about us. We believe our acceptance is dependent upon everything we do well. The less imperfections are known, the more comfortable we become. Everyone wants to have it all together. This is the reason when your friends come to you with issues or problems, you feel obligated to have answers or solutions. Most of us fail to indulge in the freedom to simply not have all of the answers our friends need in a time of distress.

I'd like to challenge your old perception by sharing some wisdom thoughts.

Firstly, self-disclosure can be a powerful tool when used correctly. It is communication that uses self to express attributes as it relates to another person or subject at hand. It's how you communicate relatable knowledge to the circumstance of another. When you use self-disclosure as a supporting tool it can make the difference in someone's hurt or healing. This is why it should be used with caution and with wisdom.

Using wisdom is the act of applying knowledge at the right place and time. Without wisdom, self-disclosure can be destructive to you and hurt those you intend to help. The reason your intended words of encouragement caused more hurt than help is that you were providing advice from your knowledge of the situation but not your heart or the wisdom that was revealed to you. You don't have to be experienced to have wisdom. Wisdom is given freely to those who ask. Who do you ask? The Most High.

I know you have vented to someone and the response you receive seemed useless because it was about them. This may include them telling you what they felt or did when they were in the same situation. Now, they have made the situation about them, and you feel minimized. This is because it has become a challenge for some of us to listen and ONLY respond when or if our response is warranted. Wisdom suggests that when self-disclosure is not useful, the most appropriate response is your attention and listening ear.

You should never strive to be the friend who has an answer to all of someone's problems. This is a street route to burnout. And in this case, your friend isn't the one to blame. You are the one to blame because you surrendered to pressure placed upon you by you. You surrendered to pressure to have it all figured out for your friend. Your wish to be a good friend could have been an opportunity for growth for your friend. Hindering a friend's growth is not a quality of a good friend, neither is enabling others and supporting their dependence on you. When you know better, you do better.

Secondly, at times you are aware that you may not be the most appropriate person to help someone through certain situations, but you still had to disguise your incapability by offering to help. Your listening ear can many times suffice. When your friend needs professional help, you should refer your friend to someone else. If your friend needs to stir up his/her prayer life, you should refer them. Because you *can* pray in for your friend, but you can't pray *for* your friend. Again, some things are out of your league, and the last thing you should want to do is try to play God in someone's life.

Don't get me wrong, I realize some of our friends expect us to have all of the right answers. But trust me, this is a notion that you have created. You can change that! Have this conversation when the time is right. Wisdom is the ability to understand differences, it will help you know when to respond or refer. Besides, this journey is about you becoming more self-aware and this is beneficial to YOU and your friend!

Be the friend you want to see. SECURE your limits, and be conscious of your boundaries. Don't minimize the importance of people and their needs by giving them a weakened version of you. Reveal to them that you are constantly learning yourself so you couldn't have answers for everything. Be grateful for the unknown; you are sure to gain experience each day you are alive. Trust me, wisdom will come, and she will let you know when and what to share and for the rightful purpose!

Day Journaling

Who am I?

Do my friends trust my advice? Am I able to listen without responding when a friend is venting to me?

Affirmations: I use self-disclosure as a helping tool, not a hurting tool. I release anything I am carrying that is too heavy to level up.

Grow Moment

Reflect on how you respond when a friend is hurting. Discuss how you normally respond and what changes you would like to make in the future.

____

____

____

____

____

Look at You GROW!

3
FRIENDSHIPS ARE SEASONED OR SEASONAL

Have you ever grown apart from someone you felt was a perfect friend? You can't explain what happened, you think something is wrong with you or the other person. Well, let me be the first to inform you, there could be absolutely nothing wrong with you and possibly nothing wrong with the friend. The reality is people sometimes grow apart. Friendships are like the feet of toddlers; they grow and grow until they have matured enough to stand alone or walk together. After a time, things may seem off in the relationship, then we naturally wonder if this is a beginning to an end. This is when we begin trying to assist the friendship back to the early stages or the stage when things were favorable. Unconsciously, we place the value of relationships on how long they remain the same. For example, someone may get married. This is a new dynamic and there are new roles added to the individual. On the other hand, the other friend may struggle and not understand the roles of a new wife. During this stage is when one or both friends are now focusing on the change; then that's when the blaming can begin. That's why it is important to have open real conversations with true friends. Especially when you're noticing a change within yourself or your friend. When there has been a change such as marriage, divorce, or death, the needs of any individual are likely to increase, decrease or

change. These moments are great indicators that the blossoming real friendship is established. This is an opportunity for growth. If your friendship can withstand these times, you have yourself a seasoned friendship.

We should take the time to establish goals in all of our relationships. When there is change within friendships and relationships, we should take a closer look at how both individuals have changed. If two individuals are growing, it is likely the relationship has also, but it doesn't mean it is growing apart.

I'll briefly describe a situation where I realized I had outgrown a relationship and the friendship couldn't continue.

This person and I became very close very fast. In my opinion, we were 100 percent in. I admired the vulnerability in this person because I was able to discern her need for true acceptance and no judgment. In my mind, I was able to give her exactly what she needed, or so I thought. After a few months in this new relationship, I began to recognize there were other needs. Specifically, one that I wasn't even physically or mentally capable of providing but instead of talking to her about it, I chose to give it the best that I could. This was a mistake. It was a mistake because I was already giving it the best that I could. Now this person that I loved and adored for the "wrong" qualities had more like a responsibility than a friend. Not to mention that all of her other friends had thrown in the towel and I was left to do what she had stated no one had ever done for her. Stay. This young lady vented about how people walked away from her and she didn't understand why. So, what did I do? Again, I made it my priority to stick with her no matter what. I wasn't going to do what the others did. I wanted to be the one who changed her view on real friends. Well as you have probably guessed, the more I decided to stay, the harder it became to stay. The relationship had become an obligation. I felt I was in an emotionally abusive relationship. It was only when I neglected to do what "she" thought was loyal to her, that the relationship ended. The funny thing was, I was trying to do what no one else had ever done and it was too much for her to accept. You see, our definitions of loyalty didn't add up and we had never had a real discussion about this. I was busy trying to be loyal and wasn't even aware of what her loyalties consisted of. This was a breakdown in the relationship that open up for real conversations she wasn't ready to have. In the end, she was the one who couldn't accept my apology for the wrong I never believed I did. This was a seasonal friendship.

I included this topic to emphasize that sometimes others expect you to be like *them* and *you* may expect *them to be like you*. This is not fair to either person. Some people aren't receptive to receive from the level of care that you are capable to give. You should never begin a relationship with the intent to prove who you are. The relationship should grow and mature as you learn more and more about a person. Have the conversations when and if the opportunity arrives. But more than anything else be careful about what you commit to doing

for someone else. Everyone who claims and affirms their personality isn't interested in who *you* are as a friend, but they are more interested in you being who *they* are as a friend.

A good friend is conscious of the expectations they have placed on others. There is nothing more loyal than deciding to be the best friend to someone else without placing your expectations on them to be *"your"* best and not their best.

Friends make mistakes and have the option to apologize but friends also have an option to accept or deny the apology.

Day Journaling

Who Am I?

Am I in a friendship that has changed? Is there an opportunity to grow from it?

Affirmations: **I am growing in, out, and through relationships and it's perfectly okay.**

Grow Moment

Reflect on your current friendship(s). Journal your thoughts about changes you would like to see.

____

____

____

____

____

Growing and Glowing!

4
You're Not a Child anymore

One of the most difficult things to overcome in our lives is judgment from people. And believe it or not, this is not completely a fault of our own. Think about it. We all wanted to make our parents proud as we grew. Then as we became older, we wanted to make our children and every other significant person in our lives proud of us. And there is absolutely nothing wrong with that. However, there is a healthy balance to this process. We must be willing to ask ourselves the best questions to understand the meaning of why we make the decisions we do. Hang on, I'm going somewhere.

As a young child, you were reminded and maybe even threatened by words *"you best get to this place and act like you have some home training"*. How about this one, *"you better not embarrass me in front of company."* Have you ever wondered what our parents were relaying? I accept how you behave when no one else is around, but when you are around *"others"*, you need to alter yourself and live up to the people's expectations until we are back in our "normal" place.

Please understand that our parents weren't doing any intentional wrong, but what they were doing is teaching a lesson that you have something to do (assigned expectation) in the presence of others. It is called assigned expectations for the appeasing of others. Parents were communicating to us, that in specific times, we need to be our best selves so people won't make judgments about you and inevitably have a notion about your personality. Wow! Isn't that the same thing happening till today? Most people that you worry about are judging you, don't know you, and are only going to accompany you for a while. These are the same people who may make instant assumptions about you based on something you wore or said or didn't wear or didn't say! Well congratulations, You're not a kid anymore. You have absolutely nothing that needs to be proven to anyone except YOURSELF. Today we will put this idea of a norm to rest. Get away from the idea that someone thinks you have it all together at all times. They actually know that you don't! One important lesson we can learn is most people will never be completely satisfied with you anyway. Truth be told, the people who are looking for complete satisfaction from someone are actually lacking satisfaction themselves. Much of the disappointment we experience from people is caused by disproportionate expectations. In order words, if you can't measure my worst or my best you shouldn't expect anything of me. A great man of God told me years ago that the higher you lift a person, the farther they can fall in your eyes. Therefore, when we are lifting others or they are lifting us, that is just an unconscious method to set us up for failure.

Just in case you are this person, allow me to let you in on a secret. Nothing is more annoying than interacting with a people-pleaser.

Constantly worrying about other people's opinions of you is not at all attractive. It is a clue to your insecurities and compels others to not trust you. I've learned if you think you are always the topic of another person's conversation then most likely your conversations are always on another person. A good method to practice getting away from discussion of others is to talk about yourself. Your accomplishments, goals and dreams. I know that can become annoying to others as well, but at least you really know what you're talking about.

Try to remember, most people won't discuss you but a few minutes anyway.

There's just so much more going on and so many other people to talk about.

Day Journaling

Who am I?

Am I constantly considering what others will think or believe about me?

Do I alter my true self to appease others?

When making a simple decision, do I always consider what if I'm noticed?

Affirmations: I am loved and accepted by the right people.

Grow Moment

GROW: Write about a decision that you have or will have to make. Talk about how you will consider making future decisions?

____

____

____

____

____

Wow, look at you GROW!

5
The Perspective

More often than not, there are two types of people involved in a conflict. There's the person who welcomes it, and then there is the person who prefers to avoid it. In the new millennium, we have normalized delegating who is right and who is wrong in almost every disagreement. But guess what…neither person is wrong or right!

Let me explain.

When it comes to conflict, we all could use more practice. We should simply learn to be more assertive. In order to be assertive, your action or words shouldn't initiate conflict, but know I'm not telling you to run from it. Simply put, let's learn to Resolve it.

It would be beneficial for you to see every disagreement as an opportunity to GROW. Most times you only see it as one person being wrong (more than likely not you). Do you ever stop to think that there are two perspectives around it? Well, your experience is what creates your perspective. And if two individuals have different experiences, then their perspectives are more than likely going to be different. This, my friend, is where conflicts arise.

So, let's talk about the person who seems to welcome conflict. There can be a few reasons why someone welcomes it. First, this may be simply all a person is accustomed to. It is a must that they disagree, perhaps a challenge even. A person who greets a challenge with open arms certainly shouldn't be automatically labeled a negative person. All of this can be determined by their response. I have met people who never agree with what the majority believes, just in hopes of striking a meaningful debate. It is their way of gaining more knowledge, or insight. This makes me think of a defense attorney. Just because they represent a client, doesn't mean they believe their client is innocent. The attorney is merely playing the role contrary to a prosecutor to determine how much is known about what was really done by their client. As they state, *"the burden is upon you to prove my client is guilty."* Personally, I love this idea.

Secondly, I am not oblivious to the fact that people can become aggressive in conflict. To be honest, this type of person likely has some major inner conflicts. If this is you, you may struggle with working things out within yourself, so it is second nature to be in opposition with every available debate. Now, I should not have to ask you not to be aggressive or to stay away from people who threaten your safety. No sane person is willing to fistfight with someone over a simple disagreement. I can recommend you surround yourself with people who at least appear sane. If you happen to have someone in particular that you always have a knock out drag out with, I am personally telling you this journal is not the complete answer. There

are resources out there to assist you or that person, but my goal is to increase your self-awareness and provide insight to what is possibly happening when you have a conflict.

Lastly, you may be a person who avoids conflict or what I label as passive individuals. You don't have a dog in the fight. This is okay until the situation really does involve you. I will admit that this kind of person can be irritating at times. But I have learned that these types of people have their reasons too. To my surprise, many passive people are ex-aggressors. In your aggressive days, you decided you didn't want to be that person any longer. You may have taken some anger management courses or something similar. Well, you are probably compensating yourself right now, and you are passive to a fault. Find your balance. Be open to listen to your friends and supporters. Your assertiveness is needed. If you remain in this place for too long, you may begin to believe you are incapable of expressing yourself. Trust me, someone is depending on you! Most of all you are depending on you!

Furthermore, the point is this, all conflict is not negative. It is time to find a median or a balanced approach. Why not make use of your intellect. Healthily argue your points. Be alert and willing to share in a healthy debate. Someone always wants to learn something new. Even if they are unwilling to admit it.

Day Journaling

Who Am I?

Who am I in the face of conflict? Am I assertive, passive or aggressive?

Affirmations: I have the ability to have healthy, productive debates. I can learn in every disagreement.

Grow Moment

Reflect on a time when you were passive or aggressive. Journal the changes you wish to see.

____

____

____

____

____

You GROW friend!

6
Flawed Or Fair

Pride is tricky. It vacillates your decisions. I am convinced that a measure of choices we make is due to our flawed pride. Flawed pride is damaged or blemished self-esteem that you hold within. It is a form of defense but also can be used as a weapon if it feels threatened.

Pride is a dual complex. Think about it this way, a lack of pride mirrors the absence of self-respect but being prideful gives the absence of humbleness. In other words, being full of pride is cocky. Simply stated, too much or too little pride is still flawed pride. Any self-awareness journey that does not address pride isn't exactly complete. Again, the goal is to assist you with recognizing yourself when there is a presence or absence of pride. So active self-awareness allows you to be aware of when you are reacting from a place of pride. It also supports a certainty you will be able to make decisions that aren't from a flawed pride and you are likely to grow into the best version of you. So, let's get into it.

If you are like I am, you have behavioral practices and personal traits that you credit your genetic makeup for. For example, you are known for your quick temper, or reputation of having a no-nonsense attitude. We like to term it, *"take no crap from anyone."* In some cases, you may excuse inappropriateness because you were *"raised"* that way. Your involvement in a fistfight might be justified by your comparison to a parent or relative who is known to be a fighter. This is especially common in minority communities. You know the saying, *"that child is just like her daddy."* I am not oblivious to the fact that there are personality traits passed down through generations of families. However, I do believe in this case that there is a cultural methodology to our reasoning rather than *"taking accountability for what we are communicating with our actions."* Think about it. If you come from a family of professionals, then you will pride yourself on being a professional. This is where pride resides, my friend.

A common situation where pride is often expressive is in relationships; or should I say courtships. The presence of pride is a brick wall for a couple. It's a physical barrier preventing cohesion between couples. In a relationship where there is a challenge, no one is willing to take the initiative to resolve it. For instance, there has been an unfaithful act committed by your partner, and even though they have asked for forgiveness, you still cannot trust them, instead of having a conversation with your partner, you stopped cooking dinner, laundry and now you're in the house slamming doors. You're responding, but you're not communicating. This is exactly how pride looks. Now your partner's response to you is sleeping on the couch every night just to avoid you. Now, you both are communicating with pride.

The evidence of a healthy relationship between partners is effective communication, this is a sign for possible dialogue. This means the communication is intentional. It wants to solve discrepancies and misunderstandings one way or another. This is the no stone left unturned method. If the relationship cannot continue, needs a break, or whatever the case may be, it is discussed and understood by both parties. That is healthy even if it hurts.

If you are hurt by someone, you should communicate by saying, "I was hurt when..." This statement is clear and has a goal. The response of someone in a relationship should resemble, *"what can I do to not hurt you again."* This response is the best and is without pride.

I am a person who believes that there is a balance for almost everything we experience including expressing pride. As stated above, the absence of pride is not flawless. You should have pride, just not to the extent that it causes you to act out an ill will.

Let's call it fair pride. Fair pride is reasonable. It can allow you to make sound decisions with pride. It is okay to be proud. The presence of your pride should not operate from offense. There are some moments when your pride aims to protect or preserve your reputation or legacy. That is the reason you need to be completely aware of your motives when you react from a place of pride. But don't fool yourself, because a legacy of beating up people is not one you should be necessarily anxious to protect!

Day Journaling

Who Am I?

Do I recognize when I am acting from flawed pride?

Affirmations: I have fair pride. My pride is a bonus to my personality.

Grow Moment

Reflect a time that you were reacting from pride. Journal the changes you wish to see.

____

____

____

____

____

You GROW so nicely!

7
Miss the Mark of Mediocracy

If you have never failed at anything, you should ask yourself if you have actually tried to accomplish much of anything in your life. I'm talking about that thing you wouldn't even let your brain ponder past the millisecond that you thought it. Yea, that thing! You do know you have the ability, right? Well, if you have ever dreamed about it, then it is within your reach. You've got to be willing to fail to get it. I'll explain.

Failures are not preferably desired, but they are essential to your hopes of accomplishing something. Failure is a flashlight that can guide you through the darkness that *it* places you in. You can use the flashlight to see what to avoid and to see other routes to take. At times you may need to use someone else's flashlight, and it can be of help. Eventually, you will still have to get your flashlight again. Let's break this down. If I borrow your flashlight, at some point the batteries are going to die. Now I can continue using it or just return it to you. But if I want to continue using it, I will need to do something on my own now. That is simply replacing the old batteries and putting in my own, "new" ones. In other words, others can give you helpful advice. Advice that can very well be of use, but only to a point. You

will need to pave your way. You need *your* mistakes, *your* failures to guide you to your destination.

At some time in your life, you will need to decide to avoid mediocracy. Mediocre is the contentment of being quiet, unnoticed, and never seeking to stand out. It's being careful not to fail. No disrespect to those who have passed away, but not attempting anything is like an unidentified dead body. It seems wasteful. It's a tragic ending for any human being. I would rather die trying than continue to live and never attempt my dream. (I literally felt chills writing that).

All of that was said just to get you to end the cycle of mediocre thinking. You need to dream. Stop being afraid of failure. Don't be content with just average. Dig deep within yourself and be honest about what it is you want to accomplish. You do not have to settle for mediocre. There is a world of possibility out there. Now all you have to do is dream BIG and work HARD.

Day Journaling

Who Am I?

What is my dream? Have I been fearful to move on my dream? Am I afraid of failure?

Affirmations: I am planting good seeds in my life and I will water them every day!

Grow Moment

Reflect on your efforts to live your dreams. Journal what changes you wish to see.

____

____

____

____

____

You GROW so nicely!

8

Self-love

Without self-love, self-awareness can easily guide you to a practice of self-destruction. Imagine going from day-to-day learning things about yourself you may or may not like, maybe some of the things you have judged someone for. It is humility that you feel after you learn most of your experiences could have been more pleasant or peaceful had you better understood the role you played. The purpose of this journey is not for you to develop guilt or shame for your imperfections, but to support your efforts to better understand your subsequent responses to the actions of others.

Self-love is important. Sometimes it is mistaken, almost every person you ask will respond in affirmation if you ask them if they love themselves. This is because self-love is believed to be natural. However, some skills that develop naturally are sometimes delayed. Self-love can be coached, and it can also be self-taught. It does share some connection with your experiences and learned ideas about love. This explains the reason we witness our loved ones being mistreated in relationships, and then make vows to never accept abuse in our future relationships. To be honest, some people are just in love with themselves. But just as there is a difference in relationships, there is a

difference in self-love and being in love with yourself. It will be helpful for you to recognize the difference.

I believe the word *in* is significant when debating love. My belief is, if you are *in* something, that means you can also be *out* of the same thing. Therefore, you should not wish to be in love with yourself, because there is a chance that you can also become *out* of love with yourself for whatever reason. You simply should not put consideration or conditions on -love. Just love you!

What does it look like to be *in love* with yourself? I am so happy you asked. An individual in love with themselves shares some of the same characteristics of a couple that is in love. These similarities are visible most of the time. This could be appearance, economic status, or popularity. They could even come off as conceited or too well put together at times. They may be known to boast and brag about themselves. And then one day, it stops. No more dressing alike, date nights, no more laughing. No more love. The relationship that was once so nurturing, so catering all of a sudden no longer exists. Then you say to yourself, *"I would have never thought?"* Now, what do you think has happened when you are no longer nurturing or catering to yourself? Could it be that you have fallen out of love with yourself? That is why there is a difference between *self-love* and being *in love with yourself.*

Self-love is a lesson someone may have tried to teach you at an early age. But more likely than not, it was either instructed by focusing on

appearances, talents, or differences. As an example, a child with a deformity may be encouraged to repeat "I am pretty/handsome" in the hope for the child to gain self-love. However, in my opinion, this only teaches the child acceptance. I'm aware that some may not agree. You can challenge this statement as you feel. Self-love is not necessarily a natural skill, and it has to mature. And it will, as you understand what love truly is. Although there are many different interpretations and definitions, until you go through the necessary steps, you may remain unclear.

Now, let's get to some steps towards self-love.

To learn true self-love, you must gain a good understanding of what love is. You do this by learning everything you can on forgiveness. (If you still need to, refer to the journal on forgiveness). When you can truly forgive, you are now moving towards unconditional love or true love. A good sign you have conquered forgiveness is feeling overwhelming peace. The peace you feel when you can forgive is a freedom unlike any other. After you have mastered forgiveness, you transition into a state of acceptance. Acceptance is the stripping away of the conditions and expectations that you place on yourself. This part is also liberating! Now that you have accepted yourself; you realize that you are your mistakes, imperfections, and faults. These are puzzle pieces of you that complete YOU! At this point, you should start to wonder how could you *not* love yourself? It is then that you are able to celebrate YOU and everything there is about YOU! That my friend is self-love.

Day Journaling

Who Am I?

Do I love myself or am I in love with myself?

Affirmations: I am a loving person who deserves to be loved fully.

My journey of self-love means giving my mind some time to rest.

I have unconditional love for myself.

Grow Moment

Write a love letter to yourself.

____

____

____

____

____

You're lovely when you GROW!

9
DON'T GIVE UP? GROW UP!

Many times, we struggle to walk away from circumstances, relationships, or people because we are fearful of at least one or two things. For the purpose of this subject, we will focus on relationships. The initial fear is the fear of failure. You may be a person with a strong morality that is aligned with qualities such as loyalty and commitment. You believe in sticking it through because you tend to measure your value on what you believe are your successes. Your perspective may be something such as quitting is a sign of weakness or a failure. You believe giving up lessens your value. You are the type that may even take it seriously when others don't act with the same characteristics; especially when the person is associated with you.

A second reason you may not want to end a relationship is, you honestly believe you can make it better. Actually, you aren't at any fault for your hopeful thinking. You have grown, you have more insight. You believe you have so much to offer. You brainstorm ideas and new approaches that you are itching to implement! You're convinced you are the game changer or that your endurance *could* change the game. In my opinion, this person is a perfect candidate for growth. Just your loyal personality and optimism sets you apart

from so many others. But I'm sorry, YOU still have something that could use a possible change! I am here to help you understand why.

There are certain times when you are giving your best, learning your lesson, and growing at opportunity. You sometimes lose heart, but you remain dedicated because you're built for the struggle. You want others (in the relationship) to get it! You spend time trying to get them excited and support them to remain. Even when you are seeing little or no results, you still believe you are being as fruitful as you can be. I can personally declare this is an overwhelming position to be in. But honestly, it is time you take a moment to evaluate yourself in this relationship. When was the time you felt good about how things were going? Can you remember the last time you were able to celebrate the fruit of your labor? Or are you constantly putting out fires? Listen, sometimes losing sight of your own needs in a relationship is providing room for your decision to stay, while diminishing your self-worth. You now remain in a relationship hoping you're somehow going to make "it" better not realizing that the situation is not making "you" better. It has started to make you bitter. Don't stay in that. Grow up from and out of that place. You are the right person with the right motives and the right commitment, but you may just not be in the right place. Create yourself in a new space! Your own space, while it is fresh on your mind! That is not you giving up, that is you GROWING up!!

The best way to distinguish giving up from growing up is to use your peace detector. When we make changes for the better, we are at peace with our decision. But when we make decisions from a place of anger, disappointment, and disrespect then that's when we are likely to give up. This is why it is important to always look for ways to be the best version of YOU. When it's a fact that you have given your best, your peace is all the evidence you will need. When you are fortunate to experience real peace, you will trade nothing for it. And peace is always worth beyond what it cost. Besides, it will only cost you a relationship that was making you bitter, not better.

Day Journaling

Who Am I?

Are my current relationships making me better or bitter?

Do I make decisions from emotions? Am I searching for peace in all situations?

Affirmations: My Peace is my livelihood and I will find it and protect it. I'm at peace with everyone, every situation and every decision. I will not bargain for anything that does not benefit me.

Growth Moment

Reflect on a relationship or situation that you may have outgrown. Recall a time when you forced yourself to remain somewhere where you were stagnant. Describe how you felt and how the situation tried to change you. Journal changes you wish to see.

____

____

____

____

It's time to GROW up!

10
A NEW CHALLENGE ALERT

These days, we love a challenge! I have the perfect one for you.

There are some things you prefer to avoid in life. Things that you certainly want to miss out on. You refuse to allow them to remain. If these things happen to show up, you are sure to find the cure. One thing that comes to mind is sexually transmitted diseases or what we call STDs. No one wants to live with an STD. Not only do you not want to live with them, but you are also embarrassed when we have them. Not to mention furious, with the person who infected you.

I didn't want to use STDs as an example but I couldn't resist the similarities. Follow along.

Certainly, as you would want to be clear of STDs you should want the same liberty of Mentally Transmitted Distortions. Did you ever consider the emotional health of those who contributed to your mental status? An MTD is defined as a belief that has infected the mind by transporting misleading or false impressions of reality. It could be as simple as a life quote that someone swore by and made use of to teach you a life lesson. Unfortunately, the person was perhaps bitter, broken, or simply emotionally unstable. You know,

like a bitter person giving you advice. This doesn't mean that you can't learn from someone who doesn't have it "all together" but it does infer that you should be selective about what you receive from others when it can affect your life.

Don't get me wrong, Some MTD's are the results of our interpretations. But even those are birthed from someplace. Just in case you are unsure of what exactly an MTD looks like, I will name a few. Some of them may be controversial to you, but I am almost sure that you will be able to recognize them for what they are. Keep in mind, MTDs are recognized when those who hear them challenge them or consciously evaluate their reliability.

A famous one I heard is *"if a man can't pay, you shouldn't let him lay."* If you honestly challenge this statement, I'm sure you will find that it insinuates that a man that wants to have sex with you, should give you money. I don't have to say anything further. If you live by this statement, you should be open to looking deeper into why you believe this.

Another one that I challenge is *'all men are the same."* Anyone who says this has to be aware that if all men are the same, then so are all women. I think you get the point. I do however believe that there are characteristics shared by all men. However, all men are not the same. I have been guilty of making this statement, but it was usually when I was bitter about a personal situation and needed to justify my man's bad behavior. In other words, if my man did it, then all men do it.

Some MTDs manifest in your mind without help from others. These are the ones you create from the inability to hold yourself or someone else accountable. Sometimes they are your refusal to admit a need for change. Therefore, you entertain the thought until it has become a disease in the mind. But just like STDs, without proper treatment, they spread until they are detected and treated. And if left untreated, you pass along the MTDs to others. At this point, the damage is already done within yourself.

The only treatment you can give to an MTD is to challenge that thought. Be clear about why you choose to accept this as a law. It's not a crime to disprove something even if granny swore by it. Granny's experiences shaped her. And even in her wisdom, she had moments that broke her, and some of these moments were even to teach *her* a lesson. Those were her lessons. Don't allow someone else's experiences to shape you. You will have enough experience on your own.

Day Journaling

Who Am I?

What MTD has shaped me? Am I spreading it to others?

Affirmations: I am shaped by my unique experiences.

Grow Moment

Reflect on an MTD. Challenge it. Journal what changes you want to see.

____

____

____

____

____

Grow some more!

11
FORGIVENESS IS HUMILITY

There are three components that cannot be ignored on a journey to self-awareness. Those are forgiveness, forgiveness, and forgiveness. Yes, you read that correctly. There are three stages to genuine forgiveness. The first stage of forgiveness is forgiving yourself. Before this level of forgiveness, comes no other. The second is forgiveness for someone who has requested it. And then there is the third forgiveness or what I like to call anticipated forgiveness.

Let's get into it.

As stated earlier, it is okay to look back and reminisce at times. Even when it hurts, remember it's there to help. But it can only help after you have been honest enough to acknowledge it, dealt with it accordingly, and taken the big step beyond it. No matter how much you try, you will never be able to fool yourself. So don't become comfortable half doing the work, or you will be left to do even more damage control. Once you have done the necessary work, you will learn to forgive yourself with less effort. Now depending on the level of offense (which is determined by you) it may take some significant time. But initiation is the only place to begin completion. This is about you, for you. Love yourself and practice your affirmations until you

believe them. Avoid negative thought practices. Take time and give yourself space. Spend time with those who complement your existence. There is no rush, so you shouldn't feel pressured to impress yourself because inevitably you will be proud of your accomplishment. Besides, you will never be capable of forgiving others until you have mastered the art of forgiving yourself, a lesson is learned when you have forgiven yourself.

Forgiving yourself is good practice. But again, it may take a measurable effort. I find it easier to forgive others by remaining humble enough to know I am no better than anyone. I have and will continuously make mistakes. But I am self-aware enough to also know I deserve no less mercy. So, I am willing to give mercy. Allow my attempt to explain this level of humility.

Notice the words *willing to give.* You have to be conscious of what you are putting out. You must remain conscious of the mistakes you have made as a friend, a spouse, or a confidant. If you are honest then it should serve you as a reminder that it is okay to extend the same grace to someone who asks your forgiveness. When someone asks you to forgive them, a measure of humility has been displayed. This is the forgiveness that you do not want to struggle giving out. There is another that requires a new level of humility.

The third or anticipated forgiveness is the one that you give a person who hasn't even expressed regret or repentance. I won't lie, I struggled with this one for a longer period than I want to say. Only because I believed wholeheartedly that anyone that didn't ask for my forgiveness, didn't deserve it! But then again, how many times have I needed to be forgiven but never asked. No one ever said an offense has to be felt by a person for it to be offensive. Let me say it this way. Every person you have offended isn't necessarily aware of that offense. Or are they? You can never be sure. Either way, you never apologized for that offense. But it is still worthy of your repentance, and you would prefer to be forgiven. You can only hope that your repentant heart can suffice for that unknown offense. This is why I am open to forgiving those who have not asked because I also have not asked! However, I am aware of things that are unknown by others, but it doesn't make my actions any more righteous.

Learn to forgive easily. There is so much freedom tied to forgiveness. And remember, forgiveness is not for the other person, it's for YOU. Trust me, you need that peace these days.

Day Journaling

Who Am I?

Is forgiveness hard for me?

Affirmations: Forgiveness is freedom, and I deserve to be free.

Grow Moment

Reflect on a time when you felt that someone didn't deserve your forgiveness. Journal the changes you wish to see.

____

____

____

____

____

Grow On Friend!

12

Purpose and Gifts

The subject of purpose is one of the challenging topics for me. Mainly because there are days when I still question if I have mastered my true purpose. But because I understand more about my purpose today than a year ago, I can share with you my journey on finding my purpose.

Purpose is the reason something exists. Simple right? But the hard part is learning the reason you exist! It's easy for you to limit your purpose to roles such as mother, wife, minister, and so on. But let's be clear, your roles include your choices. At any time, you have the option to opt-out of the roles you chose. Simply stated, you can decide to neglect your role as a mother; even after you have birthed a child. Your role as a mother is most likely a purpose, at least one of them. Purpose is what your life or existence is destined to do. That is why you had a child (purpose), but didn't choose to be a mother (role). Now, if you want to have any satisfaction from your life, you must commit and live out your purpose. The majority of our peace is dependent on whether we are living purposefully. If you can't understand this, you are more than likely not experiencing much peace at all. Not the peace available to you at least.

If you're like I was, you have pondered and prayed, but you are still left with questions about your purpose. Trust me, I know. But would you believe me if I told you that your purpose is as simple as the meaning of the word? Purpose is the REASON YOU EXIST. Think about it. Why do you exist? Stay with me now.

We are actually bigger than ourselves. Our purpose has nothing at all to do with what we alone are capable of doing in our might. It is the spirit that lies within us that gives us supernatural abilities to carry out tasks or assignments we would ordinarily be unable to perform; it's only available at the rate of our own beliefs. I'm not here to introduce you to that inner power or to proclaim to you who or what your power comes from, I can only say who mine comes from. If I tell you that yours come from the same, it still will be of no use to you, unless you believe it yourself. That's called Faith. Let's get back to purpose, our subject at hand.

I learned my purpose only after I recognized my gifts. You see knowing your purpose is the easy part, that is not so easy. It is the gift you possess that makes way for you to live out your purpose. Even when we figure out our purpose, learning to perform it makes it still a mystery. This is why we need to know what our gifts are. The only way to learn your gift is to deliberately seek it. Anticipate revelation and listen to others around you to learn what your gift is. Remember your gift to the world is what you use to live out your purpose. The sharing of your gift will always bring joy to others. You can locate your gifts in the moments when there is simple contentment; more like over-whelming peace. You may find yourself doing things that do not make you richer, prettier or smarter, but simply brings peace to you and those around you. Don't be mistaken, your GIFTS *can* provide you with all of those things. But the funny thing is, you'd do it for no compensation at all. It's almost natural to you, and you hardly recognize your efforts at times. It is that simple.

My purpose on this earth is simple. You probably share this same purpose with me, but there are specifics to our delivery. This is when your gift will make room for you and mine will make room for me. There is one purpose we all share. That purpose is to show love to everyone. However, how we live this purpose may also be different. Again, this is where gifts come into play.

If your purpose is to show love and your gift is what will give you access for you to do this, you must learn YOUR GIFT! You may ask still ask how. I'm glad you asked.

Pay close attention to how you make others smile and how you change the course of someone's day? Be observant of how you help place others in a better state. It's not limited to money or giving any tangible thing. It could be a joke, a hug, or just as simple as a smile. The saying is, "you never know how you are helping someone.". If you are still unclear about what your gift is after praying, then listen. Ultimately there will be a moment you can recognize that this must be it. This has to be MY GIFT! Listen to your friends and love ones. They are the ones who encourage you because you are your best self when you are surrounded by love and acceptance. They will always give you an insight into your good qualities. Sometimes, just your presence is peace for someone. Take notice of this and do not take these types of gifts for granted. Listen to others when they remind you of how you helped them. This process is much easier when you are surrounded by the right circle of people.

My prayer for you is to learn your gift for the world. A lot of people are depending on it!

Day Journaling

Who Am I?

What is that I do that brings peace to myself and others? What do my friends and loved ones say about my abilities?

Affirmations: I have gifts to change the world for the better. I am confident that nothing can hold me back from living my purpose.

Grow Moment

Consider how you make others smile. Write about your gifts and how you will share them with the world. Discover your purpose.

____

____

____

____

____

Grow On Then!

13
PURPOSE AND SUCCESS

Now that you are thinking about your purpose, let's go ahead and add success. To know if you have success, you must define success. If you are fortunate enough to know your purpose then you can determine when you are successful.

The journey of self-awareness is much more rewarding when you are in the habit of celebrating successes. It was not that long ago when I realized it was practically impossible for me to be successful because I had never defined what success was for me. I knew I was making progress but had no clue when I will fulfill my vision. I had an idea of success, which were visuals in my brain. Nothing special, just a generic version that included living in a mansion, more than 2 vehicles in the garage, and a fat bank account. (You know, all the "good stuff"). Then one day someone asked me what success means to me. I was humbled at my lack of an answer I had never taken time to consider what success looked or felt like to me. I had never said it aloud. ActuaIly, I believed success pretty much looked the same for everyone. I wanted what everyone else wanted. Success, nothing specific. Just the general stuff.

Talking about a narrow mind!

So, there I was trying to be successful and didn't even realize I had no clue of what it was for me.

I hope by now you know true success is gained by fulfilling your purpose.

Success does not consist of measuring yourself up to others but merely measuring yourself up to the purpose of your life. That is the mistake that is commonly made. Success is the accomplishment of a purpose. If there is no purpose, then there can be no success.

(Remember we all share one common purpose.)

When you have inhaled your last breath, almost every bad and good thing will be forgotten, but the most important question is what will I be remembered for. A couple of good questions here are *"How did I make the world better? "What will others remember, miss, or appreciate about me?"*

Being conscious of what you want for your life and why you want is a great starting point to success. But remember *your purpose* is the GPS to get you to your destination or success.

Day Journaling

Who Am I?

What is success to me?

Affirmations: I am confident that the positive actions I take will lead to lasting rewards.

Growth Moment

Journal about how you want to be remembered. Describe how you will look when you are successful.

____

____

____

____

____

You are free to Grow!

14
CONTROL-ALT-DELETE

If you are familiar with a MacBook or Apple laptop, then you know what happens when you hold the key-combination, control, alt(option), delete. You know when no command is received by your laptop, you can use this method to help it to reboot. For those of you who are not familiar, this method is normally used when your laptop freezes and won't accept any of your commands. It happens primarily when you have given the machine tons of orders, and it isn't able to respond fast enough and just decides to halt.

I don't know about you, but I have some moments when I could use what I will name a C A D. As a matter of fact, I call this exercise a self-care.

The first thing you should do is examine your idea of control. If you can be honest, you know that very little is actually controlled by you. But the one thing you are ought to fight to control are your thoughts. To take control of your thoughts you have to practice. You can get in practice by being intentional. Take notice of the things you allow to run freely in your mind. Discipline your cognitive patterns. When you find yourself trying to particularize every detail of something, you are entertaining the intruder. The intruder is the unproductive gestures that creep into your thoughts. Here you can intentionally

refuse to entertain the overload of negatives or undesired that are trying to smother you. Take a moment to evaluate what is important *for* you at this moment, not what feels right *to* you. Keep in mind that the things that are important "for" you are a necessity and not just a need.

Secondly, a CAD can provide time to figure out what your alternate options are. Ask yourself if you are motivated by your goal or are you simply working from fear of failure. I can admit I have personally experienced this type of pressure. It looks like this…. You set an attainable, planned, goal. You start towards the goal, and all you can focus on is making it to the finish line. Instead of embracing this new level you're already on, you start to focus on everything that is in your way. You know, like acknowledging haters and those who wished you to fail. Now instead of expressing gratitude, your laser is on proving the naysayers wrong. This is just part of the process and you're right to want to do so. However, you have developed new motivation, but you've worn yourself down because now you have begun to work with a fear of failure. This is the perfect time to get refocused, so don't neglect an obvious need for a reboot!

At last, it's time to delete. What are you deleting, you ask? You are deleting all of the fears, the worries, and the moments when you became distracted by the unimportant. This is your fresh start. Starting over is a fear that most of us share. But starting over isn't so bad when you can recognize the advantages you have now. You are

working from experience! Do not be deceived. You are at a higher level now, so expect harder lessons. I like to refer to these as growing pains.

If you find yourself frozen and surviving on fumes, you're more than likely due for a CAD. It's likely, you experienced a trigger before the onset, but sometimes it's hard to recognize them due to the obligations we place on ourselves. With so many obligations, it's easy to lose control and miss seeing an alternate route. You wish that you could just start over from the top, but you have put so much in that you see staring over as failure. What you do not realize is, if you do not respond properly, you risk losing all that you have accomplished so far. I like to reboot for a minimum of 24 hours. However, I know people who just require a few minutes. There is no set duration for a CAD, but a CAD is a requirement. Self-care is REQUIRED of you. If you are not careful, certain people will make you feel guilty for taking time to take care of yourself. These are the people who will get on social media and share memes about you not being there for them when they needed you. They may have called your phone once and you didn't answer. Now you're the worst friend ever. Don't allow these types of people to make you question yourself as a friend or question your decision to have a moment of self-care. At the appropriate time, let them know how important it is for you to attend to your own needs at times. Them needing you so critically at any moment may just be an indication they too need to take advantage of a CAD.

Day Journaling

Who Am I?

Am I afraid of failure? Do I perform from a fear of failure?

Affirmations: I will let go of my worries and will focus my energy on only what I can control.

Grow Moment

Take a CAD moment. Journal your thoughts about your fears. Respond to your fears and put them to rest.

____

____

____

____

____

You Grow so well!

15
CHECK YOUR POSTURE

Self-awareness is like looking into a mental portrait of yourself and recognizing exactly who's staring back. It's knowing who you are in every situation or circumstance. It's being in tune with the truest, rawest form of yourself. It's a sacred expression of your reality. Self-awareness is the result when you are consistent with checking your own self. Simply called self-evaluation.

Self-evaluation is a healthy practice that leads to growth and it is a virtue of personal advancement. This is a consistent practice that improves your productivity and effectiveness.

I believe this is one of the most significant topics in any worthwhile conversation. Actually, it's the very reason this journal was created. When I ask others where they stand as it relates to self-awareness, the initial response I receive is "*I know me, better than anyone know me*" I can honestly say that getting to know me was not necessarily a simple process. In fact, it involved some long-suffering periods of denial and some really harsh realities. I'll admit I found it easier to tell myself a lie than to admit a hard truth.

I once found it difficult to accept flattering remarks from others. I'm not saying I did not enjoy the nice gestures of some people but I did

not trust that every compliment was pure, especially if I believe that person wasn't particularly fond of me. I finally realized I was looking for acceptance in all the wrong places. Let me explain…During certain periods in my life, I had a particular choice of people who I looked up to. These people, I valued their opinions but even more, I desired their approval unknowingly. Just like any human being, I craved attention and recognition from these certain individuals. Ironically, I found that some of them could never seem to compensate me though. I religiously confessed that whatever I did, it wasn't to gain accolades. (There I go lying to myself) But I couldn't help but take notice of how it was so rare that I received a compliment from the people that I spent most of my efforts trying to impress. I often scratch my head of how these individuals would uplift and praise others but I never was given recognition. Here I am thinking I'm as real as they come! I guess I felt ignored by those whom I desired attention. This had become too deep for me. I couldn't understand! It bothered me more than I cared to say.

So, after spending too much time considering what I was doing wrong, I started to assess the people that I looked up to and who I obsessively desired to please, and most importantly, I begin to ask myself questions. Were these individuals even impressed by my offerings of the best me? Where do I get all of the energy I use to impress them? Had they even taken the time to recognize me on their own? Or was I busy trying to give them more of what they were asking? Of course not! You have no idea how hard that truth pill was to swallow. Remember, this is self-awareness so "I" needed to change. At this moment, I had a revelation. I made up my mind to check my posture. I decided to do what I call a positional reference of Myself and those who I "looked up to."

The truth is, some people in your circle appreciate your position, but they don't respect it; neither do they respect the potential you possess. They are content with you being ordinary. That's what they like most about you. But the moment you dare to be equal or superior to them, you will find out that was a deal-breaker for them. Oh, they will congratulate you when you mention a dream about writing a book, but they won't bother to encourage you to do it. Holding on to these type of people are a hinder to your success. You look to them to acknowledge your gifts but it never happens. Not only are these people you look up to, but they are people who are forced to look down on you. Who's forcing them, you ask? You are! They can't look you eye to eye and they can't look up to you because you are too busy looking up to them! (I hope you caught that). So now you're thinking, what is wrong with having someone that you look up to. Absolutely nothing if they are the right ones to look up to! And they are the right ones only when they can respect it when your posture changes!

I won't pretend the process of identifying people such as this is easy. It's pretty overwhelming. But I'll give you one clue word for a starter…. LEADERSHIP! Take a closer look at people in your life that are in a leadership position. Are they pushing you to reach for

your goals? How many times have that leader told you what you were good at? Check your leaders and those in authority over you. But don’t spend too much time looking at those around you, Check YOUR posture friend!

Day Journaling

Who Am I?

Who are those in leadership to me? How do these individuals encourage me? Does this person support my dreams and push me to reach my goals? Do they recognize my gifts and talents?

Affirmations: I'm not in a position to be looked down upon.

Grow Moment

Reflect on a time when you needed encouragement. Who was there? Who should have been there? Journal the changes you wish to see as it relates to the leaders in your circle.

____

____

____

____

____

Look at you! I love to see you GROW!

16
Emotionally Present

In the past few years or more, I've spent quite an amount of time listening to others (especially women) vent and describe their dissatisfaction with our new generation of boys to men. Circumstantially, I have gained a lot of practice and frankly have become what I call; an intake expert. I try to always give my undivided attention to what is being said, and eventually learned to zoom in even more on what is being expressed rather than verbalized. In the field of social work, we call this active listening. I have used that skill obsessively in my former career.

One main trend to stand out for me is the way modern ladies gloat and boast of their inessential need for a partner or significant other in their life. I've heard this so often that I had begun to question if there was a fault to me because I "still did" desire to be in a relationship, a healthy one. The day I decided to quit questioning myself it hit me! I am perfectly normal for desiring companionship. This is the way I was created. additionally, the very thought that someone else desired to be alone rather than in a healthy, flourishing relationship is mind rattling to me, and they are simply not expressing the truth; therefore, they are fooling themselves. At least that is what I was eventually convinced myself to believe.

I know I'm not the only one who has been inclined to the new-age woman. You know the one who makes her own money, has her everything, and always follows up with the question "what do I need a man for." My answer to that question is, "Sis if that's all you needed from him, then you don't need one." But what about intimacy, affection, and protection? Can Tracy Dogg toys suffice for those things? (Look at you Googling Tracey Dogg).

My belief is this; the new age woman is communicating a desire to be happy, and a need to experience life with an individual in a healthy, thriving relationship. You are saying you have nothing else to give to someone who doesn't take the time to attend to your emotional needs and respond to them appropriately. I believe your emotions have been shunned and misunderstood and this is how you choose to communicate the cry for attention. Your emotions have become silent, or absent.

One of the most used lines I use when listening to a person express unhappiness with their situation is "what would make you happy right now?" I'm sometimes amazed at the inability of some to provide an answer. Unfortunately, many individuals simply are not aware of what exactly would make them happy. So, if you are unsure of what can make you happy, it's really not smart. if you are expecting someone else to know but aren't able to speak what makes you happy, you are more likely going to avoid expressing yourself. This is why you feel guilty for having an emotional response in needy situations. You

eventually decide that no one cares about how you feel. This can cause you to decide to not express what it is you really want. This decision is made based on fears; it is limited self-expression. It's an unhealthy practice to control your emotions. Deciding to avoid expression is a form of hopelessness and promotes the belief that your desires can never be met.

When you decided not to express your need for love and attention you demonstrated your belief that you can't have or don't deserve love and attention.

To express yourself emotionally, you must first create healthy boundaries. This is first done by demanding those around you to accept you and everything that comes with you. You are not *in* your feelings. You're *expressing* your feelings and no one should be able to convince you that it is something flawed about it. When someone tells you to get out of your feelings, you simply respond to them that they should get into theirs, because they are important. Then if someone is not able to handle your feelings, they should just say that.

Secondly, you have to be an example of the type of person you want to be around. Your energy is a magnet to attract what you desire. If you like to be around laughter, then laugh. You can't expect people around you to be fun and outgoing if you are always envious and frowning at others. Consistency is key. If your mood changes more often, it's likely you have little control over your emotions. Most

people will feel your vibe and either match it or simply avoid you altogether.

You deserve to be emotionally expressive at all times and you should never allow anyone to rob you of that liberty. Whether it is your man, mama, or your co-worker, as long as you're not disrespecting anyone with your expression, EXPRESS yourself. Again, we should never allow our emotions to have complete control of us. They are ours alone so no one should have to suffer by dealing with them. Be your judge. When your emotions are out of order you can *"check yourself."*

Whatever you do, avoid ignoring your emotions and never allow them to be downplayed by others. Say what you feel, and mean what you say! Respectfully, of course.

Day Journaling

Who Am I?

Do I keep my emotions hidden out of fear of being judged? Do I express my emotions freely? Am I able to express my emotions healthily?

Affirmations: My emotions are a part of me, not in control of me.

Growth Moment

Reflect on a time when you felt the need kept your feelings to yourself. Journal the changes you wish to see.

____

____

____

____

____

You are free to Grow!

17
Go The Extra Mile

Have you ever been wronged by someone who you knew in the pits of your heart loved you? Crazy, huh?

You probably asked yourself "what type of love is this." The answer is simple, it's the level of love that the person is capable of giving. It isn't uncommon that an individual can't love past what they have been loved themselves. You see, love is intentional. We have to choose to show love even when we feel we naturally love someone. Love craves activity. It needs to be heard, seen, and felt.

Imagine, a child growing up in a home where a parent or both parents express love for one another. However, the child witnesses infidelity, occasional abuse, and exploitation in the home. This child becomes an adult who has normalized hurting the ones he/she loves. The cycle is bound to continue until true love comes along and breaks it by loving the unlovable. It requires a substantial amount of empathy, patience, and compassion.

I must add that coming into the Love of Christ is how the cycle ended for me. I didn't know how to love until I met Him and felt Real Love.

Please do not interpret this as justification to remain in an abusive, unproductive relationship. Remember, this journey is aimed to increase "self"-awareness. So, remain focused and carefully understand how *you* share love?

I'm almost sure you have hurt someone you love at one time or another. It wasn't because you no longer loved them. I am convinced that the reason you hurt them is that you were only able to show them love to the highest capacity that you knew how. In your subconscious, you had rationalized, *"I've been hurt by someone who loved me, so this is not unordinary."* You didn't intend on hurting the person, what you did do is intentionally "not" love past the extra mile. Most of us have indeed normalized loving others within the boundary of our decision. But what if, in every situation, we took a moment and decided to love beyond the love we have been given?

You may ask how do I know if I am loving past my own experience. Well first, you have to admit the exact truth of what you understand about love. You have to admit that there was a specific time when you were mistaken. What you were feeling wasn't love at all. The feeling was very strong but there was little or no sacrifice involved; no giving without expectation. Love always requires sacrifices. It's a liberating sacrifice. This means it doesn't dread giving at all, even when the giving feels one-sided. If you, in the past, believed that love doesn't hurt, trust me, you are mistaken. Ask Jesus. Nevertheless, love should not feel miserable. It gives you the heart to walk away or stay. One of the most misunderstood realities about love is, love is complex; that is so far from the truth. Love is quite simple when you

are intentional and willing to make sacrifices. If you find this constantly hard to do, it may be because you are *choosing* not to love. Or maybe you're just *unwilling* to go the extra mile.

Day Journaling

Who Am I?

Am I willing to love past the love that I have been given?

What sacrifices have I made in the name of love?

Affirmations: I am loved and I am capable to love even past that. I love with the intention to show love.

Grow Moment

Reflect on a time when you hurt someone you loved. Journal your thoughts on changes that you wish to see.

____

____

____

____

____

GROW on and on!

18
To Prepare or To Manage

While living in a world filled with the unknown, it's common for us to spend a significant amount of time planning. Planning for tomorrow, for the holidays, or even planning our future. It is perceived that there is a sense of safety in planning. Because preparation is smart, right? It's better to be prepared than be unprepared, correct. What if I told you that preparation is not as important as managing?

The definition of preparation is to make or be ready to do something. When we prepare, we are on the alert to initiate on-demand to a need or task. The ironic thing is that we are spending energy preparing for the unknown. Nothing wrong with preparing. Unfortunately, no matter how much we prepare we cannot adequately prepare for the unknowns. So, we must not only be preparers, we need to learn how to effectively manage such unknowns. The occurrence of some form of crisis in our lives is inevitable. When I speak of crisis, I speak of unexpected happenings in our lives. These are the things that we never expect or see coming.

The way you respond to a crisis can change you forever. And yes, change is growth, especially when it is intentional. But what about changes that arise from a crisis? Can we be intentional about the

unknowns? Of course not! The way we respond to things is a method of managing our lives. I often observe in people, three types of responses during a crisis. These responses are to flee, freeze and/or fight. A crisis, depending on its severity, can involve one or all the said responses. Every response is recognizable when we pay attention.

My goal is that you can recognize your response during a crisis. Therefore, you are better able to manage it when the situation has not allowed for planning. And when you are able to identify your response, you will certainly be more likely to grow after a crisis.

I am going to use a circumstance of a couple as an example. One has admitted to having a long-term affair outside of the marriage and has revealed that he/she is not willing to end the affair. In other words, they are contemplating leaving the marriage. CRISIS!

A person who flees during this crisis, will flee physically, mentally, or maybe even both. You may pack your bag with no real mental intention to leave the relationship. We have all been there! That subconscious hope that things will be alright when we are calm is current in mind. Let me inform you of something here. Upon your return, the crisis will be waiting there. All the flee and return has done is allow a new normal to form. And you are contemplating the next person's move to be a better one. You don't even dare to bring the fight up again. The truth is, things can never go back to normal. The normal has changed! This was not a healthy way to manage a crisis. There will be nothing but unresolved emotional encumbrances, bitterness, and guilt. The only thing you should expect now is an extension of the crisis. Remember, the spouse is not open to ending the affair. And even if the crisis is perceived to be gone, there is still a new fragile normal. As it is with all crises, this situation is manageable but only with clear communication surrounding boundaries and expectations.

Also, the person who freezes in a crisis. There has been zero conversation about what has transpired. There have been no agreements, no apologies, NOTHING. You're just stuck. FROZE! This is when you become that friend who needs someone to attend your pity party. You expect your bestie to stay on the phone and listen to you gripe and complain about how badly you are being treated. Allow me to say to you what bestie wants to say. You know I love you, but you stayed, so you must really want to fight it out. At least that is what a good friend will say. And we all have one friend who will attend the pity party just because they are miserable in their relationship. Let's not even go there!

Fighting in a crisis varies. Some fight with their words, with their hands, or with their actions. I don't have to tell you the two of these that are inappropriate. But where there is hurt, relief can be found in some awkward places. If only you knew how to look for healing rather than relief.

An example of fighting with words is belittling or insulting others with talk. It's hitting below the belt as if you can say something so awful that it will heal the hurt that you both are feeling. I'm a firm believer that, intelligent people don't spend a lot of time thinking of words to cut people down. That only fits on the schedule of miserable, unhappy people. Find you something else to do.

Fighting with our hands can only lead us to jail. And who has time for that? Fighting with your actions looks different and mirrors a great manager. This fight is a productive and effective method when responding to a crisis.

The first thing to do in a crisis is to spend time with yourself. This time is for you to evaluate yourself in the situation. After a critical analysis, you may be surprised to learn some truths that are otherwise hard to recognize. One truth is, you can never be enough for someone who has deemed you not enough already. The time you spend evaluating should help you to realize your worth, or if the other person even deserves your effort. In reality, your past experiences have already taught you there are little or no gray areas. If you are honest, you are more than capable to determine if courtship is worth savoring. Just know whichever decision you make, to fight for yourself or the relationship, you are equipped to fight. So now it's time for you to just be sure of what it is you're fighting for.

Obviously, this crisis is one of many that you may face. There are times that our resources or planning can help us to prepare for. But again, there are those that we have to respond to effectively in order to come out with our sanity still intact. I would much rather have the ability to manage than attempt to prepare. Now that you are aware, you should decide if you would prefer to be a successful planner or manager.

Day Journaling

Who Am I?

What is my initial response to a crisis? Have I managed well during a crisis?

Affirmations: I am assertive, not passive, not aggressive. I can listen even when I do not agree.

Grow Moment

Reflect on how you respond to a crisis. Talk about the managing of that crisis. Journal your thoughts about your position. Talk about any changes that you would like to see.

____

____

____

____

____

You're good to Grow!

19
Look Back and Heal

Contrary to popular belief, we should always look back from where we have come. Even driving a vehicle requires us to look back occasionally to ensure our safety. Frankly, there is purpose in our past as it is the foundation of our future. We have all heard the cliche *"forget what's behind you and focus on what is ahead."* I agree with this to a certain extent; future events aren't all that matter. You see, when you take a moment and think about where you once were, it helps you to evaluate better where you are presently. You can determine if this is where you want to remain. This determination provides you with the insight needed so that you are likely to arrive at your expected end. Think of your future like a trip. In the planning, you have to take a moment to consider what to expect when you arrive at your desired destination. It would make me pretty anxious to just go somewhere and not even give a thought about it until I get there. Our future is the same way. We should always be alert of the present. It's purposeful to have a vision and a plan for the future. BUT none of this is possible if you don't acknowledge the past. In other words, where you are coming from is as important as where you are going. You should be grateful for the experience on your side. Think of it this way, the only reason you find yourself back in a familiar, uncomfortable place is that you didn't learn the entire lesson

the first time it happened. Don't dread your past mistakes or your humble beginnings; they made you who you are today.

I know there are certain moments in your past you wish you could just erase. Certain things are worth forgetting because they only produce bad emotions. At times, these are the things that can distract you or take your focus from what you want or what you need to accomplish. It's these memories that rob us of our hope and diminish our dreams. But ignoring our mistakes or trying to erase them from our memory is not how we are allowed to move forward. Actually, it's impossible. We should not dwell on past mistakes either but learn from them. How do I do that, you ask?

The very first step to healing is acknowledgment. Acknowledge the injury the mistake has caused you. By acknowledging your faults, you are no longer captive to them. Before you realize it, the injury has become a scar.

It's still there. You can touch it and even see it but it's just a small reminder. It is your purposed past and it has no power.

Now that you have acknowledged it, it's time to transition. It's time to take a step forward and forgive yourself. Nurture your scar. Give it a little TLC. Massage it even. I mean it's not life-threatening anymore. Be grateful for the fresh start.

Forgiveness is the best gift you can ever give yourself. It is a condition of humility as you have to remind yourself you are not perfect.

However, it's worth it. No matter how hard this process gets, remember you are still growing. Congratulate yourself for the changes you are making. Practice saying the words *"I forgive me."* Believe in yourself again and walk into that freshness. You've earned yourself a new start. Stand in your forgiveness and don't allow anyone or anything to speak anything less over your life.

When you have learned how to forgive yourself it becomes much easier to forgive others.

But now comes the real reason for the healing process.

Apply it. Testify about it! Someone out there needs to hear from you. Did you really think you went through all of that just for YOU?

Day Journaling

Who Am I?
What do I dread about the past? Am I holding on to old mistakes? Do I consider myself a victim of my past? How did I overcome my past mistakes?

Affirmations: I am aware that the strength and knowledge I've gained from my experiences can help others on the same path. Sharing my successes can lift others. Sharing my mistakes can protect them.

Grow Moment

Write a message to your past on this section. Journal the changes you want to see as it relates to your past.

____

____

____

Acknowledge your injury.
Forgive yourself.
Now apply!
Grow On!!

20
SELF-WORTH

Relationships are optional, not obligatory. I know you're probably asking why did she begin with that. Well, first of all, it's impossible to increase self-awareness without discussing the existence of toxic relationships. I believe this is one of the main hindrances to healthy self-awareness. So, let's get into it. I want to make sure that where I take you next, you understand that it is intentional.

Let's talk quickly about self-worth. What does it look like? Is there a perfect definition? Yes, of course. You define your self-worth. I'll just let you in on how I determine my own and hopefully shed some light for you.

Have you ever been in a relationship where you felt you were always the chaser? And what I mean by that is you are always the one who is responding, apologizing, and making effort to stay in contact. And when there is a disagreement, you are always the first to acknowledge you were wrong. Don't take this the wrong way now. There is absolutely nothing wrong with apologizing and taking accountability when you are trying to be a better person. (Notice I didn't say "the" better person). However, if the cycle is continuous and you are always

the one to initiate solutions, then you may be involved in a one-sided relationship. And one-sided can easily transition into toxic.

You may also be suffering from little self-worth. I see this more often in single women. In most circumstances, women with little or no self-worth have taken no time to accurately measure what they are capable of bringing to the person they're involved with. This is because they have spent more time considering what can be gained from the person rather than what can be achieved from the relationship. That's why if someone reaches the milestone to perfect self-worth it would be almost impossible for them to feel safe while entertaining anything less than what is "worth" their effort or time. This is Self-Worth in the rawest form!

Self-worth always requires self-work. It is the *"work"* that one puts into themself that determines the merit of selfishness! Self-work has nothing to do with wealth, appearance or social status. In other words, you may look better because you choose to, but you will not perform at your best until you believe everything you have is what you deserve. I know right! It blew my mind, too.

KEEP READING.

Self-worth is a form of confidence. While it states that you are whole enough to co-exist with another person, it's also knowing you are an addition to whomever you choose to engage with. When you know self-worth, you never wish to overtake or diminish others. Besides, if you sense a need to do as such, you are already aware you are in the wrong company. In other words, you understand the magnitude of being the underdog in a room full of winners. The point is that You're here. right? Now that you're here, you take advantage of resourceful acquaintances. You see this as no time for competitiveness because you are busy trying to take in everything you can. Why? Because you are anxious to get back and share your experiences and knowledge with those who look up to you. All because you know you're purposeful and valued. That is my friend, the cognitive pattern of healthy self-worth.

Now that you know your worth or lack thereof, it should be clearer to you why that relationship feels more like a bad gig rather than a companionship. It's because you forgot that you have an option. You aren't mandated to stay sis! And whoever else doesn't appreciate what it is you contribute to a relationship, then it's a good thing *you* know your contribution!

We all know a single person who we murmur about. Their choice to remain single. We automatically think it's something wrong because they aren't "with" someone. Rarely, do we assume that a single person has self-worth.

No! This is not the case for everyone. Some people are full of self too. No one is good enough for a person full of self. There is almost nothing anyone can offer this person they can't "give themselves." And sadly, there are singles that actually believe this narrative. That line of thinking is extremely unhealthy and so unresolved, but that's another lesson another day. Anyhow, let's retire the narrative that self-worth is connected to a relationship. There are a few methods to build your self-worth. I am not ignorant to the fact you are not going to master self-worth by reading a few pages of a grow journal. However, my goal was to help you to better understand where you stand as your worth is concerned. Besides, this is a self-awareness journal. The more aware you are, the better chances you will seek out the resources to do the work that supports your needs and desires. I have found that the daily use of positive affirmations is a start on your journey to increase self-confidence. I have even provided some good ones throughout the journal. Take advantage.

Remember, you got this!

Day Journaling

Who Am I?

Am I involved in any relationship that hinders my self-worth?

What's a deal-breaker for me in a relationship?

Affirmations: I am more than allowed to move past the things and people who no longer bring positivity to my life.

Grow Moment

Reflect on your self-worth. Journal what you would like to see different.

____

____

____

____

____

I love how you grow!

21
What Level is Your Love

Every individual, whether man or woman, possesses a specific love level at different moments in their lives. This level of love is defined by the measure of love we are capable of giving to another. With levels of love, come expectations. More often than not, our love levels increase from one stage to the next. This depends on our experiences and whether we accept or reject what we learn through our circumstances. I'll try and break down the three.

The first level of love is the desire to receive. At this level, a person expects gifts and surprises. This person may interpret the evidence of love comes from *"receiving"*. This level is underdeveloped. Even though it may be innocent, it expresses the highest need. Need to gain, need to obtain, and need for constant reassurance. Many times, this love is learned through tradition or generational norms. For example, a man who does give his woman money or gifts must love that woman. Or vice versa, a man who gives gifts and money must love a woman. A person loving at this level has not mastered self-love and this is why so much is required of others. A young woman at this level may feel neglected when her significant other neglects to give her what she *"expected"* for her birthday.

Secondly, we have a level of love based on convincing. This love is like the first level only it needs to convince. It could be the butterflies or tingly feeling. This love requires a particular image. A person on this level wants to hold hands in public. They want others to want what they have. This person wants to convince the world,

"I love someone and they love me back." I am willing to argue this to be the level when most people get married. Because marriage is the ultimate convincer that love exists in a relationship. Many marriages fail because this level of love never matures to the next stage. When there is no one left to convince, the relationship becomes boring, or shall I say unnoticed.

Love expressed with wisdom is a form of maturing love. This love most likely understands that love is more than gifts and holding hands in public. It accepts that love isn't endless happy days. This love has the experience and a deep desire to be reciprocated but it still places no demands. This person is aware when they are in play with an alternate level. In other words, this person doesn't love someone only when it is convenient or they are easy to love. A person that loves at the level is willing to fight for the very same love in return. But at the moment they feel they are being shorted; it becomes a clear message for change. Leaving a relationship is not the first choice but because they can decipher if an individual is capable to reciprocate their level of love. Even when they love someone, they won't compromise for long because they know what they deserve. This level of love will walk

away hurting but still happy for themselves. Happy because they can maintain love even when it wasn't appreciated or reciprocated. This level of love should be the level we all want to reach. But it can only develop after you have learned *self-love.*

Day Journaling

Who Am I?

What is my current level of love?

Affirmations: I am learning that I deserve to be LOVED with the same intensity as I give LOVE.

Growth Moment

Reflect on how you express love. Talk about the presence or absence of self-love. Journal your thoughts about what changes you would like to see.

____

____

____

____

____

Here you Grow Again!

22
VIEWER DISCRETION ADVISED

We all know what promiscuity means, I hope. If you do not, take a moment to Google the term and then come back to complete this reading when you have an understanding of the word.

For a long time, I strongly believed that women used sex to receive love while on the contrary, men used sex to express love. And in today's society, it has become extremely easy to disprove my theory. My new theory is Love has nothing at all to do with why most of us have sex. If you are honest, you will admit that love is not what you want from every person you sleep with. It's a specific feeling that comes before, during, or after the climax that you crave. This is reasoning why you need sex. Let us examine a specific moment.

Recall how you feel *"during"* sex. It feels good, right? Sometimes even great! But then at times the *"during"* is not the goal anyway. Most times it was to get you to the goal- climax. Now, the climax is the main goal! You can't deny it. But how do you feel when it's over? If it's not with a person that you love, you start to wonder if it was worth it. This means that you are looking to feel loved but you settled for sex. When you imagined yourself having sex, you should have envisioned it with a specific person. If not, then you may be experiencing promiscuity.

Don't panic and do not entertain the spirit of offense. Think of it as you are on your way to being free of a secret conviction. I'm sure, there are times when you ask yourself, *"why am I sleeping with this person"*. Actually, you intended to stop it last time but the thought of that *'feel good'* moment was over-powering. It is time you admit that you like the feeling of sexual intercourse, and you normally do not discriminate on who can give you this feeling when the desire arises. You are unfortunately capable of disconnecting with a partner but connecting to the activity of a partner. Understand this, genuine feelings are from the soul but motivating feelings aren't genuine and they arise from a needed touch. The two are different. Genuine feelings are pure and without an agenda. They don't have motives or expect anything in return. Motivated feelings are an internal crisis happening. They are hazardous when there is no ability to cope. They are triggers that lead to undesired behavior. Sex is one of the behaviors. They are the same as a "fix" to drug addiction. After you come down from your high, the first rationale you make is to try to do better next time you are triggered.

Promiscuity derives from a broken place. There has been a manifestation of gray areas in your life. If you want to overcome and change this behavior, you have to understand your past and current relationship with sex. Ask yourself about what you knew about sex at the beginning and currently. Begin with your very first encounter. If that encounter was not pleasant or left you feeling guilty, ashamed, or regretful, then it's likely that your sex practices still suffer. You need to be conscious of what you learned and didn't learn about sex. If you were taught only the immoral side to sex, then this explains the negative feelings you have when you participate in sex. It could provide insight into why you have sex without discretion. The suppression of these feelings often leads to promiscuous habits. Because sex is supposed to be pleasurable, that unwarm feeling afterward, you may deem be natural. But you are wrong. There should be no conviction attached to safe, healthy, natural sex between a man and a woman. It was created to be a beautiful connection and it remains. Rape, molestation, same-sex partner experimenting, all of these things are capable of shaping your attitudes and behaviors relating to sex. Even getting pregnant at your first sexual encounter can form a unique dynamic between you and your sexual relationships. None of these is something you have to be ashamed of. You are not wrong in your desire to feel good. You're just rejecting self-discipline and neglecting the real need. The limited time that you have spent thinking about this subject has become a barrier for you. But now, you're in your safe space to do some homework. Do not continue to spread yourself thin. Understand your attitudes and practices with sex. Admit to your limited knowledge about sex. Give yourself a complete evaluation. It is necessary for your self-awareness. This may require you to dig up some ugly facts about your past. It won't be for you to suffer but for you to suffice…or simply to be enough!

Day Journaling

Who Am I?

How did my first encounter with sex affect me?

Affirmations: I have a healthy attitude, feelings, and practices with sex.

Grow Moment

Consider your knowledge about sex. Talk about how it was shaped. Journal the changes you would like to see in your attitude and practices?

____

____

____

____

____

Growth Looks Good on You!

23
Serial Offender

I do believe we all have been introduced to the term serial killer. If you are like I am, you are intrigued by tv shows, movies, and stories that detail the mind, motives, and acts of these individuals. I find it intriguing to peek into their lives while trying to wrap my mind around their savage desire to kill. It's almost as if I'm trying to make sense of their moral reasoning. But believe it or not, and as awkward as it may feel to acknowledge, serial killers in some type of cognitive approach, justify their desire to commit acts of violence. Now deliberately admitting the truth, it's likely this same reasoning is used by serial manipulators, serial complainers, or any serial demises that one commits.

To learn what your serial offense is, you have to first identify patterns your behavior has created in your life. To help your thought process, I'll use myself as an example. I discovered I had a pattern of attaching and detaching myself to certain people. I won't elaborate on the people or the reasons at this time because it would interrupt the thought process that I'm attempting to coach you into attaining. Remember self-awareness is the goal.

A serial offense is a series of acts or traits that you perpetrate unaware. They are followed by behaviors that land you in common situations.

These situations are not specifically negative, but they cause you to relive experiences over and over again. This is due to your attraction to specific characteristics of a familiar person or thing. In my case, I was attracted to a *certain* type of person.

A serial offense is not one you may find yourself to be ashamed or even ready to excuse yourself of, but they are critical for you to recognize for you to break free of when or if they produce any undesired result. Alongside a serial offense, you are likely to convey them through a personalized message. You send the message when you become attracted to a thing or person. This is simply you responding because you like what you see. Although you're not conscious of your motive. Whether the motive is innocent, is only a decision for you to judge.

Learning to own up to your serial offense is a huge milestone on your self-awareness journey. The presence of more than one is not unusual.

With this new finding of myself, I am able to enjoy new, lasting relationships and real commitments. One major misconception that I experienced during this process, was believing that just because someone was a good or decent person, they would make me a great friend. Wrong! I had to learn everyone wasn't aligned to my purpose. And just because I felt I was the epitome of a best friend; didn't mean I was assigned to be friends with that person.

True self-awareness cannot mature unless you are completely aware and actively coping with all known truths about yourself. That includes recognizing patterns of people, places, and situations that are common for you. It's just seeking revelation by the way of genuine passion.

Spend adequate time on this one. Be clear on what your serial offense is as it will help you identify some needs you may have. Dig as deep as you can and then dig even further. I hope reading this helped to spark your best cognitive reasoning. Familiar spaces can be simple for you to identify but determining the role you play in getting to those spaces is a challenge for some. Be open, honest, and if you have an accountability partner (which you should by now), talk with them. They should be able to provide more insight. Good luck.

Day Journaling

Who Am I?

What familiar places, feelings do I experience? What are some obvious patterns that are common for me?

Affirmations: I forgive myself for giving my attention to things that didn't deserve it.

Grow Moment

Reflect on what your serial offense is. Journal changes you would like to see.

____

____

____

____

____

Keep Growing!

24
THE LESSON

Recently I ran across a post on Facebook that sparked my attention. The post was an individual boasting about their decision to quit their job because of a co-worker. The post described the co-worker's negative energy at work daily. The post was lengthy and listed all justification for why quitting the job was the "bigger" person decision. They went on to talk about how, as a positive person, they couldn't continue working with a person full of so much negativity. No judgment, but as I read the comments of others congratulating and expressing accolades for this person, I felt sympathetic towards the person who made the post. I started to question (to myself of course) "if you're this positive energy, how could you allow one negative person to cause you to leave a job?" I couldn't help but think about what I would say to this person if I was a friend of theirs.

I'm no mathematician, but I do remember how to work 7+(-6) =1. And I believe this method can be easily applied to life. I'll admit; that's my perception of most parables in life. Let's try and make it make sense. If you are like me, you have moments when you are hurt by others; specifically, those you care for. If you're human, you are

tempted to remove anyone or anything who interrupts your peace or comfort.

Some individuals require you to remove yourself from because some people are content in misery and simply wishes to witness you at your weakest state. But no one should have the power to influence your decisions for sufficiency and especially your livelihood. In other words, an individual's actions and behaviors toward you should never have the capacity to minimize or hinder your personal progress. If you allow someone to determine your present state, this is you also allowing someone to determine your future or end. As you grow, you learn unpleasant circumstances aren't just to make you miserable or to have you cutting people from your life, but some of these moments arrive in your life to teach you or to cause you to grow.

Follow along.

Remember, conflicts arise from different perspectives, and when you are willing to understand another individual perspective, a resolution most likely can be accomplished. In other words, when you are fully able to recognize your role in every interaction, you are allowing access for growth to occur. This is good grounds for *you* to learn a lesson, not the other individual. Besides, who's mind can you change? Yours! Whose attitude can you change, again, only yours! When you decide to block someone from your life every time there is an uncomfortable exchange or disagreement, you are relaying that a resolution is based *upon "a person"* willingness to learn or change something about themselves. But have you considered the change requested of you? Can you change *your* mind, attitude or behavior to resolve a difference? Or better yet, can the resolution develop because of *your* changed mind, behavior or attitude?

I hope you feel that like I felt that! This is not you admitting wrong or placing yourself to blame for what happened. It simply means you understand you could consider some things. Take time to assess your feelings, attitudes, and behaviors that contributed to the disagreement. After your transparency, you may be able to justify your reaction, but remember you have an advantage and can choose differently "next time". But *this* is not a time for transferring responsibility upon another.

There are some identifiable characteristics among your hurt feelings, bad attitudes and reckless behaviors. Be more aware of how you communicate. Ask yourself if your attitude or behavior is warranted or if there is mis-representation in your communication. If you are one to avoid or ignore others after a disagreement, you need to further examine the behavior that communicates how you are feeling. If you belittle or bad mouth others, this behavior could communicate that you are rude and envious when in actuality your feelings are hurt. It is difficult sometimes to communicate raw feelings because you aren't acknowledging the feeling, so you communicate anger when you are hurt. You react defensive because your emotions are vulnerable. This is why you are more likely to strike spouse, rather

than burst into tears when you learn of their infidelity. Pride also plays a significant role here. The goal today is to get you into practice of identifying true feelings and expressing them appropriately so you will not miss The Lesson! Again, no one is here to judge you but YOU! It is important to your growth that you believe these moments aren't just coincidental, but they are trying to teach you.

Day Journaling

Who Am I?

Do I listen to others to respond or to understand? Do my behaviors reflect when I am hurt or angry?

Affirmations: I am in control of my emotions. I do not have to hurt others because I am hurt.

Grow Moment

Think about yourself in a disagreement. Journal the changes that you wish to see.

____

____

____

____

____

Keep up the good Growth!

25
THINK LESS

I do not completely disagree with the aphorism *"always think before you react,"* as it is proven to be helpful for those of us who react impulsively. However, I do believe this statement can be exaggerated and maybe even received out of context by people who swear by its validity. Truth is, some people are stagnant in their lives due to over-thinking. It is beneficial to recognize if you are a person who over-thinks. Why? Well first, because no one is exactly excited about being in the company of someone who obsesses over everything. And second, over-thinking is not a desired characteristic. It's just that it's hard to recognize it in your own-self. There are some people who are great at planning and wants to make sure everything goes as planned. This is quite different. An overthinker can also plan but will obsess over every detail until something that is supposed to be an enjoyable event becomes a regret of their participation all together.

I have been guilty of being both people at times. I am now better at recognizing when my over thinking is a nuisance or a help. I hope you can gain some insight for yourself.

Overthinkers are likely to be considered a person with impressive intellect. This person spends significant time revisiting the past and

contemplating the future. Over-thinkers revisit their interactions over and over in their head and it usually leads them to make vows and again, regrets. This is because the thinking is out of control. Instead of preparing and moving forward with a plan, you think of how you will respond if things don't work out the way you plan. You obsess in high hopes that you won't ruin something. Over-thinkers and people pleasers have similarities but their differences are detectable. A people pleaser's main goal is to make certain a specific person is "pleased" with *them*. Whereas an overthinker wants to assure that everything goes well *for* them. Additionally, a people pleaser may desire approval from a person or group, an over-thinker may be striving for perfection. This form of overthinking is not always negative and can support growth, but striving for perfection even in your thoughts, is unhealthy and can drain you, causing you to miss the importance of whatever the goal may be.

The main hindrance to an over-thinker is the obvious. Their NEED to control. Yes, this level of overthinking has the desire to be in control. The idea that you are not in control in particular moments causes you to spiral. The need to control causes you to over plan. And this is when over-thinking becomes a negative rather than a positive attribute. When the thought of losing control arises, you begin to worry and dwell about the thought until its paralyzing and leaves you unable to focus or prioritize.

I have no clear method to introduce you to cure over-thinking, but healthy self-awareness will help you identify when you are losing control of your thoughts. I recommend to learn what your triggers are, as it is a great first step.

The beginning of an accomplishment starts with just the plan to not give up. Getting things completed can be hard for someone who spends most of their time obsessively "thinking". And again, understand there is a difference in planning and thinking. Like I mentioned, over-thinkers who plan are smart people because they seek to be prepared. But planning for perfection is not smart. And if you think something is going to be perfect, you have already "thought" about it too much. OVERTHINKING!

Just in case you learned today that you are an overthinker, today is a good day to think less and to do more.

Day Journaling

Who Am I?

Where do I draw the line when I have to complete a job or task?

What motivates me to want to do well?

Affirmations: I am qualified to get what needs to be done, done. I am able to congratulate myself for a job well-done. I don't need to be perfect to be great.

Grow Moment

Consider your motives when you plan something. Journal any changes that you would like to see.

____

____

____

____

____

Growth Looks Good on You!

26
It's A Thin Line

Have you ever wondered what drives a person to do evil? More specifically, what drives a person to commit evil to another individual. Through my own self-awareness journey, I have moments when I ponder on this. I challenge myself to consider the worst about me, and I usually conclude some startling revelations about myself. One revelation I have made is that the presence of hate is always roaming the vacant spaces of our hearts. This is true because where there is no respect, there is conditional love. We all know what conditional love is, right? Conditional love is the limits we place on others before we make the final decision of whether we can accept and inevitably love someone. In reality, this is the absence of unconditional love. Let's be honest, most of us are not able to freely give unconditional love, especially to those that we have no ties to. Where there is an absence of any love, hate is aware and waiting for an opportunity to fill this void.

Hate can be formed where there is a presence of its characteristics. These characteristics include the idea of crucifixion, violation and evil wishing on others. The manifestation of hate develops from the thought or idea to willingly jeopardize the well-being of another by one or more characteristics of hate. Allow me to break this down into

simpler terms. The evil wishes you place on an individual is trying to manifest into action that will put someone at risk for danger, loss, harm or failure. Due to my goal here, I will not apologize for the exaggerated wording. I am attempting to reference hate at its peak, and hate at this level becomes almost impossible to put into words. My goal is not to label you to be someone who hates someone. However, my goal is to provide you with a non-judgement zone that you can make an honest statement about the untold thoughts that creep into your mind. You then will be able to identify when hate is attempting to form within you. If we are honest, we all know someone we "so-claim" do not care for. Even some of us are bold enough to say, "I just do not like him or her." You could have specific reason or no reason at all. You just DON'T! Well, my friend, that is the very void that hate is looking to fill. Without proper intervention, hate can certainly manifest.

Perhaps you are an over the top, loveable person. You honestly believe you could never hate anyone. I truly hope this is your truth. But if you're like I am, you are truly committed to your journey of self-awareness, and you are willing to admit that at some point, you weren't always so whole hearted. Maybe it is being revealed to you in this moment that you have never hated anyone. Isn't it still wise to recognize when a simple dislike of someone, could possibly be trying to manifest in your heart? But because you took the initiative to self-evaluate and intervene on this flaw, you are now better self-aware and able to see it as another GROW moment.

Recognizing you are human; you may now condemn yourself for your dislikes in others. Truth be told, sometimes people intentions are to get on your nerves or make your more miserable, especially if they believe you're happy while they are not. However, healthy people don't give these types of individuals the pleasure of uprooting them from their purpose.

One of the most intriguing but disturbing observations I have ever witnessed is someone finding fault in another person who is always smiling, laughing and appearing to be floating through each day like a feather in the wind. If you are irritated by another's contentment or happiness, then that is a clear indication that you are lacking the same. It's wise to be full- aware of what bothers you or makes you cringe. But more importantly, why. Simple, but not really simple at all.

Think of it this way. Hate and love are frenemies. This means they actually have something in common. Their desire to over-power the other, to be exact. Both wish to reign in our lives. It is up to you which you will allow to have providence in your life. I challenge you to choose which is more appropriate to support the legacy you wish to leave behind. Even though both will take commitment and hard work, I hope this is not a hard choice for you to make.

Be cautious of what you murmur to yourself about others. Be quick to check your own-self. Do not allow negative feelings to linger. Discuss those within yourself. Journal about your feelings; especially when they are humiliating to say aloud. Keep it real with yourself.

One main feeling to consistently check yourself for, is envy. It's one that is quick to appear when you are not content with self-worth. Truthfully, it is unfair to hold someone's success accountable for your own short-comings. Step your game up, and you'll be just fine.

Day Journaling

Who Am I?

Do I ever feel bitter about the success of someone? Do I feel others are unworthy of success?

Affirmations: I only give energy to things that add to my growth.

Grow Moment

Reflect on a time that you were displeased or didn't *"like"* someone. Journal the changes you wish to see.

____

____

____

____

____

Look at you! I love to see you GROW!

27
ARE YOU MEETING YOUR NEEDS?

There was a specific time in my adult life when one of my primary concerns was to make sure everyone I love was doing well. The most vital mistake I was making was neglecting to make sure I was doing well. If I was aware someone was having relationship problems (really any problem) I made it my business to see they knew they could talk to me no matter how long it took. I would lie next to my husband in bed talking for hours on the phone with them, as if I was able to talk their problems away. You see my intentions were well. I cared, but I also carried! What did I carry? I carried way too much of their hurt and dissatisfaction on my shoulders. I felt a need to support them through every hurting moment. All of the venting, the crying (oh and my favorite) …the why men are the way they are discussions. Almost never did I consider I haven't said two words to my husband who has worked hard all day and now can't even fall asleep in peace because I'm chattering away on my phone next to him. Boy was I naive. My whole marriage was at risk, and here I am thinking I have an understanding husband. *"He understands me,"* I would think. I was ignorantly mistaken. What I was actually doing is relaying to my own husband the message that *"he and I could wait,"* because someone else's situation is of more importance right now. He later revealed to me he lacked intimacy and attention in the relationship. Of course, I flipped the narrative and argued it was not my fault that we weren't bonding. He's the one that lays down and turn his back because he's so tired! Ha, the nerve of me. Thank God for self-awareness. I won't even go into how I was neglecting my husband needs, but I too needed intimacy! I STILL NEED IT! But at this time in my life, I didn't have time to think about what I needed. I had loved ones and friends with relationship problems to attend to. Needless to say, when I found myself empty from pouring into others, guess who was left uncared for….ME!

I know you're probably saying, it's better to give than receive or maybe you're saying, I thought we were supposed to be supportive to our friends or loved ones who are experiencing troubles in life. And yes, you are right! But not at the expense of hindering your own health. Think about it, who are you really able to help heal while your own health is declining?

Please do not think this is an exhaustive list of how I have neglected my own needs. This is just one of the critical times that I was forced to evaluate my own self! It's called self-awareness!

Now let's talk about these *"helping others"* moments. Sometimes people really value your advice. You should already be aware to why people are prone to pour their issues out to you. Are you a good listener or is it something else? Maybe you give good advice. Awesome. But ask yourself why is it good. Is it really good or is it comfortable?

Sometimes people could care less about the advice you have and probably don't even realize the measure of it. But what they do know is that you are willing to sit and listen and complain with them about the same thing over and over again with no intention of either of you initiating a decision to change or help the situation. YEP! They are draining you! Draining you! And guess what, they KNOW you will not even attempt to mention a solution. That's where the saying misery loves comfort is birthed. I don't necessarily believe that all misery loves company, but, in my experience, misery does love comfort. If you don't believe me, the next time you find yourself in this situation with a friend complaining, ask them the question "what are you willing to do to change it?" I can almost promise there will be an awkward silence and then the answer will be a blatant lie or "I don't know or haven't thought about it yet." Oh, I can't forget this one, I'm going to pray about it. Honey I could say so much about that one. Anyhow, just try it! I strongly believe you will get 1 of the 3 responses.

Of course, there are times when people just need a listening ear. But guess what, in these times, you still have to make an observation. "What, if anything can I do to help". It's simple, help if you can and don't if you can't. Listen closely for opportunity to express your interest in helping or lack thereof. There is absolutely nothing wrong about which decision you make. Remember the decision is ultimately for YOU. But what you shouldn't do is be wasteful of yours or their time. The main thing you shouldn't do, is feel guilty for not entertaining. Some days are just not the day for someone else's bad days. Besides it's 2022, you should have no intentions to attend any pity parties and definitely no interest in providing comfort to anyone's misery! Let discuss, plan and move forward! Now don't forget when you use this new response with your friends and love ones, you should always open up with "now you do know that I love you." You don't want to come off insensitive or not concerned. Although, some will receive it wrong no matter how you present it.

Now before you go checking your list of friends to decide which one you need to use this approach with, make quite sure that you check YOU. Be sure that you are not the friend that needs comforting when you are feeling self-pity. Make certain that you have healthy coping skills and isn't pouring all that pity onto someone else. If it is you, STOP. That friend does not deserve to be subjected to the worst of your days. Friends aren't just for hard times; they are for sharing good times. I challenge you to change the dynamics of friendship. The next time you are led to call and complain, call and tell them how great of a day you have had or how blessed you are to have them in your life.

Good luck. It can change the game with some people. But more than that, it can *up* the game for you. Because this is YOUR time to grow.

Day Journaling

Who Am I?

How do I neglect my own self-care to accommodate others? How do I help those who are venting to me? Am I the one hurting and need to know I'm not alone? Do people value my advice?

Affirmations: I am allowed to say NO to others and YES to myself.

Grow Moment

Write a list of things that you do for self-care. Journal what changes you would like to see.

____

____

____

____

____

Look at you! I love to see you GROW!

28
Small Feet

Have you ever grown apart from someone you felt was a perfect friend? You can't explain what happened or why so you immediately think something is faulty within you or within the other person. Well let me be the first to inform you, there could be absolutely nothing wrong with you and possibly nothing wrong with the friend. The reality is people sometimes grow apart. Friendships are like the feet of toddlers, they grow and grow until they have matured enough to stand alone or walk together.

After sometime, things may seem off in the relationship, then we naturally wonder if this is a beginning to an end. This is when we begin trying to assist the friendship back to early stages or to the stage when things were good. Unconsciously, we place the value of relationships on longevity. For example, someone gets married and this is completely new to him and there are new roles added to the individual, he has to adapt and accommodates his new status, while on the other hand, the other friend may find it hard to understand the intricacies of being a new wife. At this stage, one or both friends are now trying to adapt to these changes; and suddenly complaints and blames begin to find expression. That's why it is important to have open real conversations with true friends. Especially when you're noticing a change within yourself or your friend. When there has been a change such as marriage, divorce or death needs of any individual are likely to increase, decrease or change.

These moments are great indicators that the blossoming real friendship is established. This is an opportunity for growth. We should take the time to establish goals in all of our relationships. When there is change within friendships and relationships, we should take a closer look at how both individuals have changed. If two individuals are growing, it is likely the relationship has also, but it doesn't mean it is growing apart. This is an opportunity to become a better friend.

I'll briefly describe a situation where I realized I had outgrown a relationship and the friendship couldn't continue.

This person and I became very close within a short time. In my opinion, we were 100 percent in. I admired the vulnerability in this person because I was able to discern her need for true acceptance and no judgment. In my mind, I was able to give her exactly what she needed, or so I thought. After a few months in this new relationship, I began to recognize there were other needs. Specifically, one that I wasn't even physically or mentally capable of providing but instead of talking to her about it, I chose to give it the best that I could. This was a mistake. It was a mistake because I was already giving it the best that I could. Now this person that I absolutely loved and adored for the "wrong" qualities had more like a responsibility than a friend. Not to mention that all of her other friends had threw in the towel and I was left to do what she had stated no one had ever done for her. Stay.

This young lady vented about how people walked away from her and she didn't understand why. So, what did I do? Again, I made it my priority to stick with her no matter what. I wasn't going to do what the others did. I wanted to be the one who changed her view on real friends. Well as you have probably guessed, the more I decided to stay, the harder it became to stay. The relationship had become an obligation. I felt I was in an emotionally abusive relationship. It was only when I neglected to do what "she" thought was loyal to her, that the relationship ended. The funny thing was, I was trying to do what no one else had ever done and it was too much for her to accept. You see, our definitions of loyalty didn't add up and we had never had a real discussion about this. I was busy trying to be loyal and weren't even aware of what her loyalties consisted of. This was a breakdown in the relationship that open up for real conversations she wasn't ready to have. In the end, she was the one who couldn't accept my apology for the wrong I never believed I did.

I included this topic to stress that sometimes others expect you to be as *them* and *you* may expect *you* from them. This is not fair to either person. Some people aren't receptive to receive from the level of care that you are capable to give. You should never begin a relationship with an intent to prove who you are. The relationship should grow and mature as you learn more and more of a person. Have the conversations when and if the opportunity arrives. But more than anything else be careful about what you commit to doing for someone else. Everyone who says they are, aren't interested in who *you* are as a

friend, but they are more interested in you being who *they* are as a friend.

A good friend is conscious of the expectations they have placed on others. There is nothing more loyal than deciding to be the best friend to someone else without placing your expectations on them to be "your" best and not their best.

Friends make mistakes and have the option to apologize but friends also have an option to accept or deny the apology.

Day Journaling

Who Am I?

What kind of friend are you? Are you in a relationship that has changed and there's an opportunity to grow from it?

Affirmations: I am growing in, out, and through relationships and it's perfectly okay. I am a good friend and I attract good friends

Grow Moment

Write about a favorable relationship that you are in currently. List particular characteristics that are favorable about the relationship. Journal about your comfort when having hard conversations with the person.

____

____

____

____

____

You really did it! Happy Growth Season

Self-Awareness-Post Questions

What did I learn about me that I didn't know 1 year ago?

____

____

____

____

What am I most proud of today?

____

____

____

____

What areas are still sensitive for me?

____

____

____

____

How will my life benefit from this new self-awareness?

____

____

____

Congratulations, you have completed the journey!

This book is dedicated to my mother, Denise "The Big Den" Johnson

Continue to Rest in Love, my Queen.

Thanks to my husband (Johnny) and children (Laquanda, Deondre, Omario, and Tylan) for keeping a smile on my face and making me feel special even when I didn't believe in myself. Thanks for being patient with me when I wasn't the best wife and mother. I love you with all of my being.

Thanks to my sister-cousins Latesha and Emily, who have inspired, encouraged and supported every dream I have ever had. You two are the sisters that every cousin needs. I love and appreciate you for accepting me as your big sister.

Thank you to my entire family who is also my support team. Thanks, Rochelle (Dorothy), Monique and Bridget! You guys rock!

Rest in Love Tee-tee, "Carolee"

Latonya Denise

Made in the USA
Columbia, SC
24 November 2024